TABLE OF CONTENTS

Workbook Answers..4
  Reading: Literature & Foundational Skills 4
  Reading: Informational Texts 9
  Language 13
Practice Test Answers...26
  Practice Test #1...26
  Answers and Explanations..26
  Practice Test #2...33
  Answer Key and Explanations...33
Additional Bonus Material...40

Workbook Answers

Reading: Literature & Foundational Skills

The Alligator and the Squirrel answers

1. c
2. It was astonishing because it was very dangerous -- the alligator was very likely to catch the squirrel and eat him.
3. c
4. d
5. He let the squirrel go as a reward for making him laugh when he suggested that a tiny squirrel could help a mighty alligator
6. b
7. ne glect ed
8. a
9. b
10. a

Audrey's Braces answers

1. She thinks they will make her ugly and that other kids will ridicule her and won't want to be her friend.
2. four
3. c
4. Trojans
5. Audrey
6. Audrey's dad
7. d
8. (answers will vary) she was so happy that her friends
 still liked her and she wasn't going to be an outcast that she forgot about the little bit of physical pain she had.
9. e ven tu al ly
10. a

The Big Cupcake Heist answers

1. c
2. The word *heist* usually means a robbery of something of great value, and the word *great* implies a big event, too, but since we're also told that it's all about a cupcake, we know the author is being humorous.
3. b
4. She is being **sarcastic**, which means she is saying the opposite of what she really means.
5. perfect pumpkin pastries
6. b
7. You would stress them more than the rest of the words.
8. c
9. a real mystery
10. Probably because she knew who ate the cupcake
11. He was making a joke about Jack being dressed like a pirate and Jaci being dressed like a nurse.

Anna Beth's Birthday Party answers

1. d
2. b
3. Because she knew it was Anna Beth's dad at the door
4. accomplish – it means to do, achieve, make happen, etc.
5. answers will vary

Josh's Big Game answers

1. ant i ci pa tion
2. c
3. d
4. a
5. d
6. un der es ti mat ed
7. c

8. it means they looked at each other at the same time

9. (answers will vary) they were concerned because Josh wanted to get back into the game and they wanted to make sure that didn't happen | they were each waiting for the other to speak | they knew how disappointed Josh was and wanted to choose their words carefully |

10. c

11. the fact that it was the conference championship game

12. d

13. Yes, because he can't wait 'til next year.

14. Dr. Huff

15. b

Meagan's Trip answers

1. The first meaning refers to the trip Meagan is taking to go hiking on Mount Ellis. The second meaning refers to her tripping over the root and breaking her arm.

2. Happy Valley Humane Society

3. animal doctor

4. vet er i nar i an

5. b

6. dry runs

7. a

8. c

9. She fell and broke her arm because she was running so fast she didn't notice the root and tripped over it. She was running in order to catch up to the others because she had stayed behind to take a photo.

10. preventing

11. (several possible answers) *skipped*

each takes place during an outdoor athletic event (football game, hike)

main character suffers serious injury

characters are mainly young people

each involves a group of friends (football team, Girl Scout troop)

a long awaited day doesn't turn out the way the person had hoped it would

- 6 -

the main character is sad at first after being injured, but later cheers up thanks to friends

the main characters find out how much their friends care about them

12. The difference was that they were playing in a conference game, for the season championship. They couldn't quit playing, or they would have lost the game, and the championship. The best way to show Josh how much they cared for him was to keep playing and win the game. In the other story, the girls can come back to Mount Ellis and hike any time they want to.

A Boy and His Best Friend answers

1. (any two)
Travis calls his parents Ma and Pa
Ma drives a wagon, not a car
Travis attends a one-room school house
2. She means he has to do them every day and not get behind on them.
3. c
4. showering him with soft, wet kisses
5. Chance was Travis's shadow
6. b

Zeus vs. Typhon answers

1. the phrase *fate was with me that day* means that Zeus won the drawing to become ruler of the gods
2. b
3. dis guise
4. c
5. a
6. (any three) hurling thunderbolts, flying through the sky on winged horses, flames shooting out of the mouth of Typhon, 200 knives in Typhon's mouth, instant reattachment of toes and fingers, picking up a mountain and throwing it on Typhon, etc.
7. she is the goddess of wisdom
8. Tartarus

- 7 -

9. momentarily
10. a

Jack's First Christmas in Africa answers

1. He had to get used to eating strange food, and living in a hut
2. a maze ment
3. she meant she didn't really believe him when he said he was fine
4. He said *"fine, I guess"*, which doesn't sound like he means it, and he sighed
5. cb

The Big 6th Grade Election answers

1. tallied
2. c
3. throw in the towel
4. to give up; to quit
5. answers will vary

Reading: Informational Texts

Gabby Douglas: Star of the Olympics answers

1. The Olympics
2. c
3. Opinion. That the Olympics take place every four years is a fact, but whether or not it's the most prestigious sports event is a matter of personal opinion. Millions of people would agree that the Olympics competition is the most prestigious sporting event in the world, but it is still an opinion, not a fact.
4. contagious
5. a family who allows someone from out of town to stay with them for an extended period of time
6. endorsement deals
7. ten
8. maneuver
9. c
10. d

Gabby Douglas: My Story answers

1. She would probably say no, because it was seeing her big sister doing gymnastics that led her to start training at such a young age.
2. Liang Chow
3. (answers will vary; here are some possible answers)
Gymnastics training is very hard
Training several hours a day is not only hard, but very boring
She missed her real family and old friends
She was injured or sick
She didn't think she was good enough to become a champion
4. This one. The other article is more focused on the Olympics and Gabby's previous accomplishments in gymnastics, but this article gives us more insight into what kind of person she is and the background she came from.
5. a

The Wonderful World of World Records answers

1. athletics
2. new records are set every year, so the book needs to updated with the new information
3. b
4. answers will vary
5. a

All About New Zealand answers

1. Lake Taupo
2. c
3. No. It is in the Southern Hemisphere, near the South Pole. America is a very long distance from New Zealand, in the Northern Hemisphere.
4. Hawaii
5. b

Earthquakes and Volcanoes in New Zealand answers

1. Answers will vary
2. 2006
3. February 3, 1931
4. 20 km
5. The previous article was written to encourage people to visit New Zealand. People tend to be scared of earthquakes, so if they knew that New Zealand has a lot of little earthquakes they might decide not to visit.

Metamorphosis answers

1. one
2. No
3. b
4. the leaves they're born on ("leaves" is also acceptable)
5. no

6. pupa

7 chrys a lis

8. Monarch

9. b

10. fas ci nat ing

11. cocoon

12. No; the baby may get around differently, but it has not changed into something completely different looking.

How to Make Spaghetti answers

1. not necessary; not required

2. following a good recipe

3. a

4. a bowl with holes in it for draining liquids from foods

5. it does not say how many servings the recipe provides

Weather Can Be Dangerous answers

1. c

2. take part | take part | engage

3. b

4. A blizzard features extreme cold and strong winds, in addition to snow.

5. c

Roger Staubach: Football Legend answers

1. d

2. c

3. con sec u tive

4. Most Valuable Player

5. to fulfill his obligation to serve in the Navy

6. the Heisman Trophy

7. d

8. answers will vary

No Ordinary House Cats! answers

1. intriguing
2. exotic
3. cheetahs; the article says they can outrun any animal over short distances
4. the jaguar; the article says no other animal can compete with its power
5. No
6. in trigu ing
7. re tract a ble
8. dies because it can't breath
9. the context is talking about the cheetah getting food by grabbing an animal around its throat
10. to inform--the article has elements of both entertainment and information, but its main purpose is to inform

Language

It's All Relative answers

1. Whoever
2. where
3. whom
4. when
5. who or that
6. which
7. Whichever
8. how
9. whose
10. that
11. where
12. which
13. which
14. how
15. that

Progressive Tense Exercises answers

1. I am watching TV.
2. I am riding my bike.
3. I am washing my hair.
4. I am eating lunch.
5. I am playing chess
6. We were sleeping when the thunderstorm started.
7. We were studying for the test because we didn't want to fail.
8. We were swimming in the deep end of the pool when the lifeguard announced the pool was closing.
9. We were reading quietly when the teacher announced a surprise quiz.
10. I was watching videos on my phone when the battery died.
11. will be playing
12. am going to be studying

13. will be watching
14. will be traveling
15. are going to be arriving

Modal Verbs Exercise answers

1. can
2. might
3. may
4. should
5. would
6. must
7. must
8. Can
9. cannot (or can't)
10. could
11. must
12. must
13. could
14. ought to
15. will

Adjective Order Exercise answers

1. d
2. a
3. b
4. c
5. d
6. c
7. c
8. a
9. b
10. a

Preposition Exercise answers

1. in
2. to
3. by
4. in
5. regarding
6. of
7. under
8. around
9. on
10. down

Find the Prepositional Phrase answers

1. before you leap –ADV
2. into things – ADV
3. across the nation – ADJ
4. in time – ADJ
5. of prevention – ADJ
6. after lunch – ADV
7. during the test period – ADV
8. between two opinions – ADV
9. except for Lawanda -- ADJ
10. off the couch – ADV

Complete Sentence Exercise answers

1. Stop right there
2. gave her grandmother a hug
3. enjoyed reading that book
4. are coming over tonight
5. think that's incorrect
6. ran a 10k
7. is 14 years old

8. revolves around the sun
9. is awesome
10. is taller than Jim

Fragment or Complete Sentence Exercise answers

1. F
2. C
3. F
4. F
5. C
6. C
7. F
8. F
9. C
10. C

Run-on Sentence Exercise answers

1. R
2. R
3. C
4. C
5. C
6. R
7. C
8. R
9. C
10. R

Homophone Exercise answers

1. principal
2. flour
3. four

4. too
5. whole
6. waste
7. it's
8. its
9. to
10. there
11. right
12. weight
13. steel
14. they're
15. two
16. stare
17. piece
18. bear
19. brake
20. son
21. hour
22. their
23. pour
24. plain
25. pair

Capitalization Exercise answers

1. NO CHANGE
2. That's Easy for You to Say!
3. Cheaper by the Dozen
4. Chicago, Illinois
5. I would like to make an appointment with Doctor Jones
6. "Be careful, Frank!" yelled Coach Johnson.
7. After the game, a reporter interviewed the coach.
8. Last year on vacation, we went to Yellowstone National Park.
9. NO CHANGE
10. Muslims believe in Allah and follow the teachings of the Koran.

11. Bill Gates was the founder of company called Microsoft.
12. My great-grandfather fought in World War II.
13. Christmas and New Year's Day are always one week apart.
14. Dear Reverend Swanson,
15. In my opinion, no salad is complete without Italian dressing.

Commas and Quotation Marks Exercise answers

1. "Do you know what time it is?" the little girl asked.
2. "That's strange," thought Cindy, "the puppy was just here but now he's gone."
3. Mrs. Rojas said, "Please raise your hand if you're still working on the test."
4. Mom asked, "Who wants to help me with the dishes?"
5. Bonnie said, "I think that's the best field trip we've ever been on."

Coordinating Conjunctions Exercise answers

1. I'm a light sleeper, but my sister is a very deep sleeper.
2. I play soccer, and I am becoming a better player every year.
3. Do you want to play checkers, or do you want to play chess?
4. It was raining very hard, so I grabbed my umbrella.
5. We went to the zoo, and we went to the art museum.

Spelling Exercise answers

1. c
2. a
3. a
4. b
5. d
6. d
7. b
8. b
9. a

10. b

Being Concise Exercise answers

1. I arrive at school every day at 8 AM. | I arrive at school every weekday at 8 AM.
2. During the California Gold Rush
3. Joe was smiling because he passed the test.
4. If it starts raining, we'll go inside.
5. There are 50 states in America. | Currently, there are 50 states in America.

Connotation and Denotation Exercise answers

1. b
2. d
3. a
4. d
5. c
6. d
7. a
8. b
9. c
10. c

Using Punctuation for Effect Exercise answers

1. The three Rs--reading, 'riting, and 'rithmetic--form the foundation of education.
2. The big game--the one I've been telling you about all week--starts in exactly one hour.
3. As the crowd cheered him on, Rico bent his knees, swung for the fences--and struck out.
4. I can't believe I got a 100 on my math test--a 100!
5. That's the first 100 I've ever gotten on a math test--actually it's the first 100 I've ever gotten on any test.

6. My favorite author--the only one whose books I read again and again—is J.K. Rowling.

7. Four teams are left: Chicago, Dallas, New York, and Los Angeles.

8. There's only one person who can save us: Superman.

9. I only ask for one thing, class: that everyone does his or her best.

10. I had to make a decision: go to Ann's house after school, or go to Brenda's house.

11. They lost again today; that makes 20 games lost in a row.

12. It's half past five; Grandma and Grandpa should be here any minute.

13. It looks like rain; I'd better take an umbrella.

14. This is Tony's classroom; Tammy's classroom is down the hall.

15. We have to arrive at school early; we're going on a field trip.

Formal and Informal English Exercise answers

1. F
2. I
3. F
4. F
5. F
6. I
7. I
8. F
9. I
10. I

Vocabulary Exercise 1 answers

1. pupil
2. agriculture
3. fortunate
4. auditorium
5. population

6. assist
7. vertical
8. lecture
9. recognize
10. accomplish
11. curiosity
12. suggest
13. slender
14. mature
15. superb
16. seldom
17. pleasure
18. compassion
19. massive
20. admire

Vocabulary Exercise 2 answers

1. hesitate
2. annually
3. tremble
4. plead
5. biology
6. boundary
7. companion
8. thrifty
9. elevate
10. tarnish
11. circular
12. decrease
13. quench
14. foreign
15. furnish
16. request
17. coarse

18. environment
19. predict
20. absent

Greek and Latin Roots, Prefixes and Suffixes answers

1. earth
2. far
3. body
4. measure
5. heat
6. small
7. many
8. write
9. star
10. life
11. year
12. carry
13. bend
14. all
15. see
16. speech
17. sound
18. excessive
19. opposite
20. not

Similes and Metaphors Exercise answers

1. Trent turns into a bulldozer | Trent turns into a strong person who runs other players over
2. like a dream come true | it was something I had wanted to do for a long time
3. as white as a ghost | very, very pale

4. The Yankees are the 800 pound gorilla | the Yankees are a very powerful team others are afraid of

5. he's a vacuum cleaner | he eats so much it's as if he just vacuums food into his mouth

6. like a big blue blanket | the sky covers the whole world

7. Just like clockwork | the cat is as reliable as a clock

8. you're a magician in the kitchen | Mrs. Jones is an extremely good cook

9. like a giraffe | Sam was much taller than the others, so he stood out

10. You're an angel | you're a very nice person

Idioms Exercise answers

1. telling a person something that's not true but pretending that it is
2. promising
3. someone who talks tough, but really isn't
4. raining extremely hard
5. extremely expensive
6. got very angry
7. someone who spends a lot of time on the couch
8. going out of your way not to make someone angry or unhappy
9. wait; calm down
10. in trouble

Proverbs Exercise answers

1. the mice will play
2. home
3. before they hatch
4. louder than words
5. catches the worm
6. deserves another
7. and eat it, too
8. in one basket
9. are soon parted
10. the eye of the beholder

Antonym Exercise answers

1. hideous
2. inferior
3. rare
4. stingy
5. friendly
6. boring
7. seldom
8. temporary
9. loyalty
10. folly
11. slow
12. clumsy
13. shame
14. failure
15. liquid
16. organized
17. close
18. dislike
19. dull
20. weakness

Synonym Exercise answers

1. frailty
2. regal
3. prize
4. thing
5. leap
6. anxious
7. hilarious
8. depressed
9. shrub

10. ocean
11. total
12. cyclone
13. purchase
14. powerful
15. rock
16. foolish
17. squirm
18. city
19. intelligent
20. sleepy

Practice Test Answers

Practice Test #1

Answers and Explanations

1. B: The Land of Oz. The Witch of the North refers to "this Land of Oz" and the great desert that surrounds it. The exact quote is: "'The North is my home,' said the old lady, 'and at its edge is the same great desert that surrounds *this Land of Oz*. I'm afraid, my dear, you will have to live with us.'"

2. A: Return to her aunt and uncle. Dorothy says she wants to return to her aunt and uncle because they will be worried about her. She asks the Munchkins and the Witch of the North to help her. The passage states: "Dorothy carried the shoes into the house and placed them on the table. Then she came out again to the Munchkins and said: '*I am anxious to get back to my aunt and uncle*, for I am sure they will worry about me. Can you help me find my way?'"

3. D: Sad. Dorothy feels anxious and sad about her situation. Her emotions are evident when she begins to cry: "*Dorothy began to sob* at this, for she felt lonely among all these strange people. Her tears seemed to grieve the kind-hearted Munchkins, for they immediately took out their handkerchiefs and began to weep also."

4. B: She suggests that Dorothy ask the Wizard of Oz for help and gives Dorothy a kiss for protection. The Witch of the North says: "Then you must go to the City of Emeralds. Perhaps Oz will help you." At the end of the passage she gives Dorothy a kiss: "'No, I cannot do that,' she replied, 'but I will give you my kiss, and no one will dare injure a person who has been kissed by the Witch of the North.' She came close to Dorothy and kissed her gently on the forehead. Where her lips touched the girl, they left a round, shining mark, as Dorothy found out soon after."

5. C: To ask the Wizard of Oz for help. The Witch of the North says: "Then you must go to the City of Emeralds. Perhaps Oz will help you." Dorothy asks, "How can I get there?" The Witch of the North replies, "You must walk. It is a long journey, through a country that is sometimes pleasant and sometimes dark and terrible. However, I will use all the magic arts I know of to keep you from harm."

6. A: Cry. Students should use context clues to determine that Dorothy's tears cause the Munchkins to create their own tears.

7. B: Nice. Students should use context clues to determine that the word pleasant means the opposite of "dark and terrible."

8. B: "How do I find the City of Emeralds?" Dorothy asked the Witch of the North. Before Dorothy can begin her journey, she needs to know how to find the City of Emeralds. Choices A and C tell what might happen later in Dorothy's journey. Choice D is a question Dorothy might ask, but it is not necessary to beginning her journey.

9. D: "Stay right beside me, Toto," said Dorothy nervously to her little black dog. This sentence best conveys Dorothy's feelings of anxiety at being in a strange land and beginning what is sure to be a difficult journey. The other sentence choices are statements of fact (Choice C), opinion (Choice B), or a practical statement that does not express any particular emotion (Choice A).

10. A: Dorothy followed the yellow brick road through the green countryside dotted with little blue houses. This is the only sentence choice that describes the setting of the story for the reader. The other sentence choices describe what Dorothy does (Choice B) and how she feels (Choices C and D).

11. C: Finally, Dorothy came upon a shady tree and sat down under its leaves to rest. Students should use the transition word "finally" to signal that this event happens after Dorothy has been walking for a long time. The other sentence choices indicate events that might happen before Dorothy started her walk (Choices B and D) or during her walk (Choice A).

12. B: Dorothy was tired after her long walk and soon fell asleep. This is the only sentence choice that follows naturally from the previous events in the paragraph. The other sentence choices describe events that might have occurred earlier (Choices A and C) and how Dorothy and Toto feel (Choice D).

13. B: How to set up an aquarium. The main idea of this article is the beginning basics of setting up an aquarium.

14. A: Tropical freshwater species. The article states: "Tropical freshwater species are the easiest fish to keep because their needs change based on their surroundings and the resources they have available. They are able to adapt to living in different environments."

15. D: Choose your fish. The article states: "Choose your fish first. This will tell you what type of tank, water, and plants you need."

16. C: Tropical freshwater species. The article states: "Some tropical freshwater fish include the rosy barb, angelfish, and x-ray fish."

17. B: To change in order to fit in. The preceding sentence and this sentence together give the reader the context needed to understand the word: "Tropical freshwater species are the easiest fish to keep because their needs change based on their surroundings and the resources they have available. They are able to adapt to living in different environments."

18. C: If my fish usually live in schools, how many of that kind do I need? This answer choice asks the author to expand on information given in the article: "If the type of fish you chose normally live in schools, or groups, that means they are social fish. You will need to buy more than one of that kind to keep your fish from being lonely." The other answer choices are off topic (Choice A) or ask for information about fish that is not directly related to setting up an aquarium (Choices B and D).

19. B: Butterflies are interesting and beautiful insects. This is the best answer choice because it is a general statement that tells what the paragraph will be about. The other answer choices are detail sentences that give additional information about butterflies.

20. A: A butterfly is an insect with a thin body and four wings. Choice A is the definition of a butterfly. It gives more information about what a butterfly is than the definition in Choice C. Choices B and D are details about butterflies, not definitions.

21. D: Another example of a butterfly that is poisonous to eat is a Monarch butterfly. This is the best sentence to follow the sentence given: A Pipevine Swallowtail butterfly is poisonous to eat. Choice A is a description of butterflies, Choice B repeats information already in the given sentence, and Choice C gives information about the butterfly's life cycle.

22. C: During a process called metamorphosis, a caterpillar changes into a chrysalis and then an adult butterfly. This sentence gives the most information about the life cycle of a butterfly. Choice A gives some information about the butterfly's life cycle, but the information is not as complete as it is in Choice C. Choices B and D give other information about butterflies that is not directly related to their life cycle.

23. B: A butterfly drinks flower nectar through a tube in its mouth called a proboscis. Choice B gives the most complete information about a butterfly's eating habits. Choices A and C give information about a butterfly's eating habits, but not as much information as Choice B. Choice D gives information that is unrelated to a butterfly's eating habits.

24. C: Butterflies are insects that begin life as caterpillars, change through metamorphosis, and eat flower nectar through a tube called a proboscis. This is the only answer choice that provides a summary of information about butterflies.

25. D: Nonfiction (true) biography. This is the best choice for the most information about Abraham Lincoln's life. A dictionary (Choice A) would tell you who Abraham Lincoln was, but it would not give you detailed information about his life. A thesaurus (Choice B) is a book of synonyms and antonyms and would not give you any information about Abraham Lincoln. A fiction (made up) short story (Choice C) might be about Abraham Lincoln, but since it is fiction (made up), you could not be sure that the information was true.

26. B: Childhood, Adulthood, Greatest Accomplishments. This answer choice includes three important categories of information about Abraham Lincoln: his childhood, his adulthood, and his accomplishments as president. Choice A has childhood and adulthood, but also includes favorite foods, which is not an important category. Choice C includes only categories from Abraham Lincoln's early life. Choice D includes two categories of information that may be interesting but are not important: favorite foods and hobbies.

27. A: Abraham Lincoln was born on February 12, 1809. This is the only answer choice that includes information from Abraham Lincoln's childhood. All of the other answer choices have information about Abraham Lincoln's adulthood.

28. D: Timeline of events in Abraham Lincoln's life. Although all of the other choices would give information about Abraham Lincoln, a timeline is the best choice for a biography because it would show the important events across the entire span of Lincoln's life.

29. C: stammered nervously. The sentences should read: "I don't like being the center of attention. I can't get up and speak in front of all of those people," Peter stammered nervously. The context of the sentence indicates that Peter is nervous.

30. B: which. The sentence should read: The movie, which was about a baseball player, started late. The part of the sentence set off by commas "_____ was about a baseball player" is a nonrestrictive relative clause. The sentence can stand on its own without this clause: The movie started late. If the sentence could not stand on its own, the commas would be removed and the word "that" would be the correct choice.

31. B: will be. The sentence should read: I will be taking the bus to school tomorrow. Based on the context of the sentence, which indicates a time in the future, the correct answer is the future progressive tense: "will be taking."

32. D: field, Friday. The sentence should read: Our class is taking a field trip on Friday. Days of the week are capitalized. Field is not capitalized unless it is at the beginning of a sentence.

33. B: too, to. The sentence should read: The bookshelf was too high for Daniel to reach.

34. A: vacation, January. The sentence should read: We are going on our family vacation in January.

35. A: "May I go to the movies with John tomorrow?" Sam asked his mom. Speech belongs inside quotation marks. If the speech is a question, the question mark belongs inside the quotation marks, as shown in Choice A. The part of the sentence identifying the speaker belongs outside of the quotation marks.

36. C: Molly, watch out for the runaway train! The sentence is an exclamation, a warning to keep away from the runaway train. This calls for an exclamation point.

37. D: Maria wanted to give a party for her mom, and she wanted it to be a surprise. A comma is used before the coordinating conjunction "and" in this compound sentence.

38. B: Enemy. The word ally means a friend or someone who is with you for a common purpose. Enemy is the opposite of ally.

39. C: Spoke strongly against. The context of the sentence should be used to determine the meaning of the word protested.

40. D: Brag about your accomplishments. The word boast means to brag about your accomplishments or talk about yourself with pride.

41. B: Friends bring color and happiness into our lives. Friends are the flowers in the garden of life. This is a metaphor saying that life is a garden and friends are the flowers in that garden. Flowers bring color, beauty, and happiness to everyone who sees them. In the same way, friends bring color, beauty, and happiness into our lives.

42. A: Always think about your actions before doing anything. "Look before you leap" means stop and think before you take action, considering the consequences of your decisions in advance.

43. B: (väl' ən tir'). This part of the dictionary entry tells how to pronounce the word volunteer.

44. D: september. The sentence should read: Margaret and I are hoping to attend the comic book convention next September. The names of months are always capitalized.

Practice Test #2

Answer Key and Explanations

1. B: Mary is looking for a garden no one has seen for ten years. The following lines indicate that Mary is looking for a mysterious garden that no one has seen for ten years: "Perhaps it led into the garden which no one had seen for ten years. As she was not at all a timid child and always did what she wanted to do, Mary went to the green door and turned the handle. She hoped the door would not open because she wanted to be sure she had found the mysterious garden."

2. A: Curious and bold. This passage shows that Mary is curious because she is looking for a garden that no one has seen for ten years. She is bold because she opens doors without worrying that she might not be allowed to do so or that there might be trouble on the other side. From the passage: "As she was not at all a timid child and always did what she wanted to do, Mary went to the green door and turned the handle."

3. D: An orchard. From the passage: "She hoped the door would not open because she wanted to be sure she had found the mysterious garden—but it did open quite easily and she walked through it and found herself in an orchard."

4. D: "Oh," exclaimed Mary. "It looks just as I imagined it would!" Based on the passage from *The Secret Garden*, Mary is curious and determined. She is drawn to the mystery of the secret garden and is consumed with finding it. She is unlikely to immediately share her discovery with other people (Choice C), express disbelief (Choice B), or be unsure what she has found (Choice A).

5. B: The branches of the trees were empty of leaves, but had been allowed to grow into and around each other, like a woven roof blocking out part of the sky. The garden has not been tended in ten years, so anything that had been planted would have long ago run wild and not still be in neat rows

- 33 -

(Choice A). Choices C and D describe what Mary thinks, rather than what she sees.

6. A: Mary had finally found what she had been searching for. This is the only answer choice that brings the events of the paragraph to a conclusion. Choice B continues the action of the paragraph, Choice C continues the description of the garden, and Choice D describes Mary's thoughts before the events of the paragraph.

7. C: A garden where the flowers are trees for tiny fairies. This poem compares a garden of flowers to a forest of trees. The flowers are as big as trees to the tiny fairies that take shelter under their petals, as described in the poem: "Tiny woods below whose boughs / Shady fairies weave a house."

8. B: A garden of flowers with a tiny fairy sitting under them. The poem compares a flower garden to a forest and says that the flowers are like trees for tiny fairies.

9. D: in lines that are not complete sentences and form verses. The sentences should read: The ideas in the passage are expressed in complete sentences that form a paragraph. The ideas in the poem are expressed in lines that are not complete sentences and form verses. This is the only answer choice that correctly identifies the differences in structure between the passage and the poem.

10. A: the trees are bare and the grass is dead. The sentences should read: The poem has a vibrant setting filled with blooming flowers. The passage describes Mary in a setting where the trees are bare and the grass is dead. The passage says: "There were walls all round it also and trees trained against them, and there were bare fruit-trees growing in the winter-browned grass."

11. C: Both selections are about the secrets that a garden holds. Mary is looking for the mysterious garden that no one has seen for ten years. The bird seems to be calling to her to find out the secret of the garden. The poem describes a flower garden as a forest for fairies and implies that only children can know this secret.

12. B: third person, first person. The sentence should read: The passage is told in the third person, and the poem is told in the first person. The poem's author refers to himself as I (first person): "Where, if I were not so tall, I should live for good and all." The passage author speaks *about* Mary (third person): "Mary made no response."

13. D: Comparison of two sides of a question. This article presents both sides of the question: should kids have chores?

14. A: Having chores teaches skills and responsibility while children help their parents. This is the best choice to paraphrase all of the information on the PROS side of the chart. The information includes: "Chores teach responsibility and skills that children can use later in life" and "Chores allow children to help their parents and contribute to their families."

15. C: Chores give them a feeling of contributing to their families. The article says: "Other kids said that they didn't mind having chores because it made them feel they were contributing to their families."

16. B: Chores can teach kids skills and responsibility and allow them to help their families, but can also take away kids' freedom and time for other things. This is the only answer choice that includes all of the information in the chart.

17. C: The author doesn't like chores and plans to never give his or her kids chores to do. The article begins with: "It seems all I ever do is chores," and ends with: "When I have kids, I'm never going to make them do chores."

18. D: Making the bed makes it difficult to get to the school bus on time. The article says: "Making my bed is hard when I am trying to rush out the door to the school bus. There just isn't enough time. It's like my parents want me to be late."

19. C: Trash smells bad. As stated in the article: "Taking out the trash is even worse. It really stinks!"

20. C: secondhand, firsthand. The sentence should read: The first article is a secondhand account that presents both sides of the issue, and the second article is a firsthand account that talks only about the author's own experience.

21. A: should have chores and why they should not. The sentence should read: The first article, "Should Kids Have Chores?" gives reasons why kids should have chores and why they should not, and the second article, "Chores, Chores, and Chores!" gives reasons why kids should not have chores. The first article presents both sides of the issue.

22. B: It is important for kids to take on the responsibility that chores provide. This is the only answer choice that provides a general statement in favor of kids having chores to do.

23. C: Kids should have chores in order to teach them valuable skills such as planning and preparing a meal. This is the only answer choice that uses a linking phrase "in order to" to connect an opinion with a reason for kids to have chores. Choice A is an opinion without a reason. Choice B is a list of chores. Choice D is an opinion that is not in favor of kids having chores.

24. D: A study by XYZ Enterprises showed that kids who have the added responsibility of chores receive higher grades in school than those who do not. This is the only answer choice that contains a fact that supports the idea of kids having chores. Choices A and C support the idea of kids having chores but are stated as opinions rather than facts. Choice C is an opinion that is against kids having chores.

25. C: Kids should take on the responsibility of chores to help their parents, learn new skills, and perform better in school. This is the only answer choice that summarizes reasons kids should have chores. Choices A and B do not state that kids should have chores, which is the focus of the paragraph. Choice D does state that kids should have chores to do, but it does not summarize the reasons why kids should have chores.

26. B: *What Is Happening to the Sea Turtles?* This is the only title related to endangered animals. Choice A is about machines, Choice C is about plants and flowers, and Choice C is about dogs.

27. D: Sit quietly and listen to the report, then ask questions at the end. The appropriate behavior in this situation is to give your full attention to the person speaking and wait until the report is over before asking questions.

28. A: Small group discussion with other students. This is an example of informal speech that is appropriate for a small group discussion.

29. B: Spoken (oral) report in front of the class. This is an example of formal speech that is appropriate for a spoken report in front of the class.

30. C: exclaimed excitedly. The sentence should read: "I can't believe that I won the science fair!" Rachel exclaimed excitedly. The context of the sentence indicates that Rachel is excited.

31. A: May. The sentences should read: I really want to read that book. May I borrow it? Since the first sentence indicates that the speaker wants to borrow the book, the second sentence should be asking permission to do so.

32. B: big old. The conventional pattern for adjectives indicates that size comes before age. The sentence should read: "Are we going to stay in this big old house?" I asked my mother.

33. D: near. The sentence should read: Amber likes to shop in the grocery store near the school. "Near the school" forms a prepositional phrase that modifies "the grocery store." Although Choices A, B, and C are also prepositions, they do not make sense in the context of the sentence.

34. C: Whose. Whose is the possessive form of the word and indicates that the teacher wants to know to whom the paper belongs. The sentence should read: "Whose paper is this?" the teacher asked.

35. C: Virginia, spring. The names of states are capitalized. The names of seasons are not capitalized. The sentence should read: We are going to take a trip to Virginia this spring.

36. A: banquet, competition. The sentence should read: There will be a banquet after the competition to recognize the winner.

37. D: leaped. Although "got" and "stood up" (Choices A and B) could complete the sentence, the best choice is "leaped" since the first part of the sentence indicates that Jackson is so excited that he can't control his actions. The sentence should read: Jackson was so excited to be elected class president that he leaped out of his seat.

38. B: Because he could not be trusted to behave, Jonah had to sit next to Mr. Harvey during the school assembly. All of the other answer choices contain sentence fragments, rather than complete sentences.

39. D: May I have some cake? This is an interrogative sentence and so should end with a question mark.

40. C: Marcus was glad this test was over, but he was nervous about tomorrow's test. A comma is used before the coordinating conjunction "but" in this compound sentence.

41. A: The number of people in a place.

42. B: To write down a report or explanation of something. The Latin root "scrib" means "to write." The meaning of this root word combined with the context of the sentence indicates the meaning of the word describe.

43. D: A group of musicians who play together. Context clues within these sentences include references to Sam's violin and Diane's flute.

44. C: Wet. Moist and wet are synonyms of each other.

Additional Bonus Material

Due to our efforts to try to keep this book to a manageable length, we've created a link that will give you access to all of your additional bonus material.

Please visit http://www.mometrix.com/bonus948/ssmcag4readwb to access the information.